I LIKE WEIRD ANIMALS!

Weird Birds

Carmen Bredeson

Series Science Consultant:
Dennis L. Claussen, PhD
Professor of Zoology
Miami University
Oxford, OH

Series Literacy Consultant:
Allan A. De Fina, PhD
Dean, College of Education/Professor of Literacy Education
New Jersey City University
Past President of the New Jersey Reading Association

CONTENTS

Words to Know

burrowing (BUH roh ing)—Living in a hole in the ground.

enemy (EH nuh mee)—An animal that tries to kill or is a threat to another animal.

nostril (NAHS trul)—A hole in the nose for breathing and smelling.

tortoise (TOR tuhs)—A type of turtle that lives on land.

weave (WEEV)—To twist straw, thread, or grass together.

WEIRD BIRDS

Birds live all over the world.

There are big birds and small birds, loud birds and quiet birds.

Some of the birds in this book do strange things.

Some look strange.

Which bird is your favorite?

This is the most dangerous bird in the world. It is called a cassowary (KA suh wair ee). With one kick, it can kill its enemy.

KIWI

A kiwi has a long, thin beak.

It is the only bird that has **nostrils** at the tip of its beak.

A kiwi sticks its long beak into the dirt.

The bird can smell worms and insects to eat. YUM!

DARWIN'S FINCH

Giant **tortoises** get a lot of bugs on their skin.

The tortoise stretches out its long neck.

Darwin's finches pick the bugs off the neck and eat them.

The tortoise gets a cleaning and the finches get a meal.

WEAVER BIRD

These birds **weave** grass and straw together.

They build huge nests at the tops of trees and telephone poles.

The big nests look like haystacks.

Each nest is home to hundreds of weaver birds.

FiELDFARE

Fieldfares (FEELD fairs) have a special way to get rid of an **enemy** bird.

They gang up and make it fly to the ground.

Then the fieldfares fly into the air and drop POOP on the bird. Splat. Splat.

The enemy bird flies away.

This fieldfare fights a blackbird for food.

fieldfare

This killdeer pretends to have a broken wing.

KILLDEER

An enemy gets close to a killdeer nest.

The parent jumps up and runs away from its eggs or chicks.

The parent flops around on the ground as if it has a broken wing.

It cries very loud.

The enemy is led away from the nest to chase the "hurt" parent.

Cuckoo

A cuckoo lays an egg, but not in her own nest.

She lays the egg in the nest of a different kind of bird.

Then she flies away.

When the little cuckoo hatches, the other birds feed it.

They think it is their baby bird.

This wren thinks the big cuckoo chick is its baby.

FRIGATE BIRD

Male frigate (FRIH git) birds try to get female birds to look at them.

The male blows up its red throat pouch.

It gets BIGGER and BIGGER.

It looks like a red balloon.

The pouch can be as big as your head.

BURROWING OWL

A **burrowing** owl hears something behind it.

Does the owl need to turn its body around to see what is there?

No! It can turn its head all the way around to its back.

It is looking for an enemy, such as a snake or a skunk.

LEARN MORE

Books

Holub, Joan. *Why Do Birds Sing?* New York: Dial Books for Young Readers, 2004.

Malyan, Sue. *Birds*. New York: Dorling Kindersley, 2005.

Sjonger, Rebecca, and Bobbie Kalman. *Birds of All Kinds*. New York: Crabtree Publishing Company, 2005.

LEARN MORE

Web Sites

Enchanted Learning
http://www.enchantedlearning.com/subjects/birds/

National Geographic
http://animals.nationalgeographic.com/animals/birds.html

INDEX

For my weird siblings: Ralph, Jack, and Renee

Enslow Elementary, an imprint of Enslow Publishers, Inc.
Enslow Elementary® is a registered trademark of Enslow Publishers, Inc.

Copyright © 2010 by Carmen Bredeson

Library of Congress Cataloging-in-Publication Data

Bredeson, Carmen.
 Weird birds / Carmen Bredeson.
  p. cm.—(I like weird animals!)
 Summary: "Provides young readers with facts about several strange birds"—Provided by publisher.
 ISBN-13: 978-0-7660-3124-1
 ISBN-10: 0-7660-3124-1
 1. Birds—Miscellanea—Juvenile literature. I. Title.
 QL676.2.B725 2009
 598—dc22
                     2008021498

Printed in the United States of America

10 9 8 7 6 5 4 3 2 1

To Our Readers: We have done our best to make sure all Internet Addresses in this book were active and appropriate when we went to press. However, the author and the publisher have no control over and assume no liability for the material available on those Internet sites or on other Web sites they may link to. Any comments or suggestions can be sent by e-mail to comments@enslow.com or to the address on the back cover.

Every effort has been made to locate all copyright holders of material used in this book. If any errors or omissions have occurred, corrections will be made in future editions of this book.

Photo Credits: © Christope Courteau/naturepl.com, p. 18; © Dani/Jeske/Animals Animals, p. 10; © Ian Wyllie/Animals Animals, p. 17; © Jan Carroll/Alamy, pp. 2, 5; © Kim Taylor/Minden Pictures, p. 13; Robert E. Barber/Alamy, p. 14; © Staffan Widstrand/naturepl.com, p. 21; © Torsten Brehm/Minden Pictures, p. 11; © Tui DeRoy/Minden Pictures, pp. 6, 9 (both).

Cover Photo: © Tui DeRoy/Minden Pictures

Note to Parents and Teachers: The *I Like Weird Animals!* series supports the National Science Education Standards for K–4 science. The Words to Know section introduces subject-specific vocabulary words, including pronunciation and definitions. Early readers may need help with these new words.

Enslow Elementary
an imprint of
E⃥ Enslow Publishers, Inc.
40 Industrial Road
Box 398
Berkeley Heights, NJ 07922
USA
http://www.enslow.com